The Last Girl

Also by Rose Solari

Difficult Weather
Orpheus in the Park
(poetry)

A Secret Woman
(novel)

Looking for Guenevere
(drama)

The Last Girl

Poems

Rose Solari

Alan Squire Publishing
Bethesda, Maryland

Alan Squire Publishing

The Last Girl is published by Alan Squire Publishing, an imprint of the Santa Fe Writers Project.

Copyright © 2014 Rose Solari.

Library of Congress Cataloging-in-Publication Data

Solari, Rose.
  [Poems. Selections]
  The last girl : poems / Rose Solari.
     pages ; cm
  ISBN 978-0-9848329-5-8 (pbk. : alk. paper)
  I. Solari, Rose. Then. II. Title.
  PS3569.O497A6 2014
  811'.54—dc23
                          2014005441

ISBN: 978-0-9848329-5-8

Jacket design by Randy Stanard, Dewitt Designs, www.dewittdesigns.com.
Cover painting by Lisa Montag Brotman, *Pink Balls*.
Inside jacket photo by Matthew Pritchard.
Copy editing and interior design by Nita Congress.
Printing consultant: Steve Waxman.
Printed by RR Donnelley.

First Edition
Ordo Vagorum

Acknowledgments

Thanks are due to the editors of the following publications in which these poems, sometimes in earlier versions, first appeared:

Gargoyle: "The Last Girl," "Who, What, When," and "Another Country"; *Innisfree Poetry Journal*: "Boy on a Cross," "Somewhere Between Four and Five A.M.," and "To the Wine-Taster"; *OCHO*: "Persephone at the Train Station" and "Island, With Goats"; *Poet Lore*: "That Day"; *Poetry Northwest*: "Myself When I Was There" and "Math and the Garden"; *The Potomac Review*: "To the Scholar of Mary Magdalene" and "Tree House of the Dream Child"; *Nth Position/ Eyewear Poetry Press Blog*/UK: "Rochelle's Movie" and "Tree House of the Dream Child"; *Truck Poetry Blog*: "Another Shore," "After All," and "Spell for Vanishing."

"A Prayer" first appeared in the anthology *The Poet's Quest for God* (Eyewear Books, 2014).

"Math and the Garden" also appeared in *Initiate: An Oxford Anthology of New Writing* (Kellogg College Centre for Creative Writing, University of Oxford, and Blackwell Books 2010).

"To the Wine-Taster" also appeared in *The Poet's Cookbook* (Bordighera Press and Purdue University, 2009).

"Making" was also issued as a promotional broadside by Blackwell Books for the 2009 Oxford Fringe Festival.

I would like to thank the Maryland State Arts Council and the National Endowment for the Arts for a grant that made the completion of some of these poems possible.

Thanks are also due to friends in the magical city of Oxford, England, where many of these poems were written. I am particularly grateful to Priscilla Tolkien, who first invited me to read there; to Rita Ricketts, who brought me into the World Writers at Blackwell Books reading series; to Clare Morgan, founder and director of the Kellogg College Centre for Creative Writing at the University of Oxford, who arranged for my time there in 2012 and opened so many doors; to the poets Jane Draycott, Jane Griffiths, and Jamie McKendrick for their wisdom and camaraderie; to the ever-supportive Back Room Poets, particularly Deborah Mason, David Olsen, and Kathleen Quinlan; to Sally Dunsmore, Director of the Oxford Literary Festival; to Chris and Ginger Andrews of Chris Andrews Publications Ltd, great publishers and fabulous hosts; to Steve Hay and Mark Pritchard, my U.K. brothers in arts; and to Monica Payne, ministering angel and dear friend.

And as always, deep thanks are due to all the members of the ASP/SFWP team, and to Jimmy Patterson for his incomparable companionship and support.

For Grace Cavalieri and Ken Flynn

Nothing is final, Dorothy thought pragmatically, and made a final decision.

—A. S. Byatt, *The Children's Book*

Table of Contents

I.

Then

Tree House of the Dream Child

It has been here forever. Who
built it, nobody knows. Time itself

might have pressed these boards
into rows, hammered home

the nails. Nobody plays here.
Neighborhood boys once hung

their pennants from its windows,
while girls slipped hand over hand

up the rope ladder. How high
the grass grows — no one lives

around here anymore. Come
with me as I walk the perimeter

of this field, and don't be afraid.
Though the earth is wild, nothing

can hurt us here. And if we're lucky,
if the light is good and a thousand

other elements conspire, we might see,
moving inside the one high room

of the tree house, the dream child. Hear
the floorboards singing her step, see

her old, new face. Safe in those walls,
plying her solitary art, she is a word

for keeping and losing, a talisman
against this sky, which is red-black,

now, and terrible, and our own.

Math and the Garden

It's all a matter of threes or fours,
like when my father died and it was
him and me and what he called god
and what I called whatever it was

that was next, only please not yet.
God won, which means that even if
he doesn't exist, He does. And Dad does
too, as river or beagle or five-year-old

prodigy writing his serious stanzas
in Latin. Which means, I guess,
that meaning is already here.
But I'm losing track. What I wanted

to say has something to do with
the dogwood, its four-petaled,
center-white blossoming that I want
every year to be more extravagant

than it is. As if the garden could be
compensation for some self-rising sap
that thins, the green seasonally less
insistent under the bud, despite all

that fertilizer and mulch. After the last
light rain in somebody's yard, the stars
disbelieving themselves, what I saw
on his face in that light was judgment

and then some. *Please*, I'd ask him.
Tell me again. I'm listening now.

Persephone at the Train Station

Pale from the indoor life
       of winter, she glides to the top

of the moving stairs, blinks back
       the sun. A bag in each hand —

one small, one heavy — she makes
       her slanting way to the concrete

island, where other travelers shift
       and mutter. She'd forgotten how

the daylight world, here, spins
       swiftly by. Beside the fountain, where

nymphs and goddesses pour water
       from jar to jar, a pair of teenagers

strum guitars and sing something
       about a hill, about climbing high above

the city. *Grab your things*, the chorus goes,
       I've come to take you home. The word

charges her heart two ways at once. In between
       is where she lives. When the white sedan

rounds the circle, her shoulders lift, then
       fall, as if pulled by sky-strung cords.

The door swings open, a woman's voice
        glints out, *My girl. My girl.* She is swept

up and in. As they pull away,
        her eyes return to the young couple,

who, above the roar of pouring
        water, begin another song.

Young Couple at the County Fair

They've already passed the pregnant woman,
crouched and pleading, trying to bribe
her sulking toddler with funnel cake.
They've left behind the shooting gallery boys,
aiming their toy rifles at a plastic sky.
Inside the bubble of their delight, they sway
through the crowd, sleek, and snagging
the envious eyes.

               If she were any
other girl, she might think it's fate,
how easily she fits under his draped arm.
If he were another boy, the night wouldn't
gleam, as now, at the turn of his head.
He is all of his body, while she has at least
two minds — one here, one leaning
a little away to watch the spinning moment,
rimmed in lights, as it settles in the air
around them and passes by.

Boy on a Cross

Street Performer in de Vargas Park,
Santa Fe, New Mexico

Out here, the desert pours in all directions
from its center of infinite, dry love. To the east,
the blue agave surrenders its thick blades; turn north,
and the cooler air tumbles between the pines
like a running boy. In this park, you might once
have surprised your own reflection in the creek,
now only a raveling memory of where water
used to be. You prefer to look up, anyway, leaping
to ride a metal cross into the sky.

                    Did you practice for this
on the football field, swinging your new-muscled body
up to pull the goalposts down? Did you hurdle
the living room couch, no one at home? Now,
in this city of dust and yellow light, you work selling
incense and tin icons, spend afternoons in the park
with friends, or at least, people who dress
like you. But you've got something over the other boys,
strumming their windy lyrics.

Surprise is part of it. First
you're here beside us, letting the tourists gather. Then
you crouch and spring high into the thinning air.
Your whole weight catches on your clawed hands
and you hang, trembling, your face turned away
like a child's from an unwelcome adult embrace. *Look*,
somebody says, *it's the boy who crucifies himself.*
On the ground, clumps of sage scuttle by like pilgrims
toward the promise of healing water. Above us,
the clouds shift to let the pitiless sun come down.

Desert Light

*In the 19th century, Western settlers in the United
States advertised for two kinds of women to join
them: potential brides to share their labors and bear
their children, and potential nuns to teach them.*

1.

In place of memory, silence
that grows inward until the heart
is hollow. A receptacle. This

is what she wants. Once
there had been a houseful
of things — servants and silver,

her mother's needlework, soft
carpets, the shining surface
of the piano. There had been

young men, with bright,
self-loving eyes. It had seemed
to strangle her.

　　　　　　She imagined
the nuns in their solitary beds,
their cool white robes, their
clean-swept lives. She thought,

That, for me?

　　　　　　Then she said, *Now.*

2.

Her family loved her, they did not
know what was wrong with her. They had
ideas — humors, aversions, female

trouble. They did not listen. As a child,
she had been the most obedient, had
entertained herself with books. And now

this willfulness. She will not ask
permission, she will go where everyone goes
who fits nowhere else.
                    She goes west.

3.

In place of appetite, an empty
cup. A sky big enough to hold
whatever it was she was waiting for.

4.

This light is mercy, though it twists her
like a wick. At night, a chip of ice
to the lips is ghosted with the old
green world. There, her mother slices
peaches into a bowl, stirs in the cream,
a shower of sugar. Here, she kneels
on a stone floor, says her novena. There,
the gray Atlantic rinses the shore

outside the window. Here, she must cross
the square each morning with buckets
of heavy water. There, the sun is a silver
muted slant. Her mother draws the blinds.
Here, there is light that could score
the soul. She has come to find if
they might match, the inner life
and the outer.

     Both dry. And both ablaze.

5.

In place of self, a scoured hollow
as the sun burns out her weakness. The desert
is made for this — first the body sweats
itself out, then the will. *Christ our Lord
spent forty days in the desert, tempted
by the devil.*
     She was twice past that
when it happened, knew the lightness
of no self, the state of grace, they call it,
fullness of an empty heart. This is the place
she knew existed before she saw it, a child
of sun born wrongly into a land of rain. Crossing
the square she cannot help herself. She stops
at the center, spreads her arms in the light, and spins.